Copyright © Dr. Tiffany Jean Quinn, 2023
All rights reserved.
ISBN: 9798865998518

Learn more about the anthology's compiler!

Dr. Tiffany Jean Quinn

Ladies and gentlemen, allow me to introduce Dr. Tiffany Quinn, an accomplished individual whose journey in the world of social work and life coaching is truly inspiring. With a rich background encompassing 18 years of valuable experience in school settings, clinical practice in outpatient clinics, and a strong diverse career path, Dr. Quinn has proven herself to be a multifaceted professional dedicated to the betterment of individuals and communities.

Dr. Tiffany Quinn's unique journey unfolds with social work being her third career, a testament to her unyielding commitment to personal growth and professional development. In this remarkable transition, she discovered her true calling and embarked on a path that has not only impacted her own life but has touched the lives of countless others.

Dr. Quinn's career path is a testament to her versatility and dedication. Her experience in the school setting has allowed her to understand the complexities of young minds and the pivotal role that support, and guidance play in their development. As a therapist and case manager in an outpatient clinic, she has been at the forefront of addressing mental health issues and providing invaluable assistance to those in need.

Beyond her clinical work, Dr. Tiffany Quinn is an entrepreneur, a published author, and the visionary founder of "The Unseen Hero Anthology" project. This project reflects her profound commitment to shining a light on those individuals who often go unnoticed, the unsung heroes in our communities who work tirelessly to make a positive impact. Through her writing, entrepreneurship, and this empowering initiative, she demonstrates an unwavering dedication to uplifting and empowering others.

Dr. Quinn's work is a testament to her passion for making a difference and her relentless pursuit of personal and professional growth. Her story is one of resilience, adaptability, and a deep-seated desire to effect positive change. It is with great pleasure that Dr. Tiffany Quinn has a book to teach and share her insights, experiences, and wisdom, knowing that her journey is a source of testimonies for all who aspire to make a lasting impact in the world of any helping professional, especially those who are struggling in their careers.

Introduction

Welcome to the "Unseen Heroes Anthology." The stories in this book are written by people who do really important things, but they are not always in the spotlight. I call them "Unseen Heroes" because much of their work has been done behind the scenes, but their work has made a huge difference in their communities.

As you read these stories, take a moment to think about the people in your life who might be like these Unseen Heroes. Maybe it's someone you know, or maybe it's you!

So, when you read these stories, remember that they are about real people. I hope that these stories inspire you to appreciate the heroes around you, and maybe you'll even want to write your story someday.

Enjoy the stories and let them inspire you to work and write about your life and remind people that trials are followed by triumphs.

Grateful,
Dr. Tiffany Jean Quinn

Preface By Dr. Tiffany Jean Quinn

In this chapter of my book, "Unseen Heroes of Social Work," I want to emphasize the incredible superpower of love, pain, purpose, courage, grit, and determination to drive us forward. My journey was a challenging one, especially when it came to pursuing higher education. Discrimination and limited income made it tough to see a way through. I spent a lifetime working hard to make ends meet, facing numerous obstacles along the way.

Changing direction and deciding to go back to school and start over was no easy task. It was during this critical phase that my mom played a pivotal role in pushing me forward, insisting that I needed to return to school.

In my anthology, I'm taking a straightforward look back at my life, transforming a story from facing trials and grief into a celebration of my triumph in education. I had to dig deep within myself during this journey, and it was a real challenge.

It's important to mention that this anthology doesn't just reflect my journey but the journeys of many others as well. I'm fortunate to have the contributions of my publisher and eleven fellow individuals who have helped compile this anthology, each bringing their own unique stories and perspectives to the narrative. These contributions serve as a testament to the collective superpower of love, pain, purpose, courage, grit, and determination that empowers us to overcome adversity and become unseen heroes.

Acknowledgments

I would like to express our deepest gratitude to all those who made this anthology a reality.

Authors and Contributors:

To the talented contributors who poured their hearts and souls into these amazing stories that fill these pages. Your dedication to the work is truly inspiring.

Publishing Team:

To Tammy Johnson, who believed in the importance of this anthology and worked tirelessly to bring it to the readers, your expertise and commitment are deeply appreciated.

Historical Social Work

The Profession

Jane Addams and Ellen Gates Starr pioneered social work with a focus on community, education, and advocacy. The contributions of Mary Ellen Richmond to professionalize social work. The development of social work schools and curricula. The First establishment of organizations like the American Association of Social Workers.

The "Unseen Hero Anthology" focuses on the community and empowerment. There are three important levels to this work.

First, at the micro level, we have passionate people who help individuals or families one-on-one. They make a big difference in people's lives.

Then, at the mezzo level, there are agencies, organizations, and formal groups. They come together to tackle bigger community problems.

Finally, at the macro level, we talk about social action for change and building strong connections within groups to solve issues. This helps the whole community.

This anthology honors the heroes at all these levels. They work hard and make the world a better place for all of us.

Build Superpowers by Connecting

In the quiet corners of our lives, where the spotlight seldom shines, there are heroes who go unnoticed. These unsung champions don't wear capes or masks, but their actions make a world of difference. They are the caregivers who tend to the sick, the teachers who ignite young minds, and the volunteers who selflessly give their time.

Think about that nurse who works long, exhausting hours, holding the hands of patients in their most vulnerable moments. Their care and compassion are the unsung heroes of the hospital ward.

Consider the teachers who inspire and empower students, often facing challenges with limited resources. They are the unsung heroes of our educational system, shaping the future one lesson at a time.

And let's not forget the volunteers who, without any expectation of recognition, dedicate themselves to making their communities better. These individuals are the unsung heroes who exemplify the spirit of selflessness and kindness.

Unseen heroes are all around us, quietly making the world a better place. They are the embodiment of the belief that it's not the grand gestures, but the everyday acts of kindness and service that truly define heroism.

Table of Contents

Learn more about the anthology's compiler!

Dr. Tiffany Jean Quinn...............................2

Introduction...5

Preface By Dr. Tiffany Jean Quinn.............7

Acknowledgments 9

Historical Social Work...............................10

The Profession 10

Dedication...16

The Looking Glass Self By Maicee Ann
Sharon Hill 25

Direction Forward By Monsiou Dimerson,
MSW...43

Madness to Miracles, Living Unleashed,.......
By Shanta Smith, MS, BSW, CSS...........................58

Totally Stumped: Turning Pain into Passion
By Katie Colding, LCSW 71

My Beginning: My Pain, My Trauma
By Dr. Kent Key, Ph.D., M.P.H 86

A Journey from Anger to Love By
Regina A. Baker, LMSW 103

From Hardship to Victory By Darcele M. Cole-
Robinson, LLMSW. 127

Informed by Experience ....

By Marcus Batson 133

Say G.R.A.C.E.

By Ayana M Fordham, MA, LCSW 145

Dedication

Kourtney La Franklin Jones

It is my honor to write this tribute about my baby boy Kourtney "Teddy Bear" Jones—a cherished son, a loving brother, a fun uncle(funcle), a devoted husband, a great nephew, and a dear friend to many. Kourtney's passing left us with a void that can never be filled, but today, I am thankful to celebrate the incredible impact he had on our community. Kourtney wore many hats in his lifetime, and in each role, he embraced, he left an Impressionable smile.

As a son, Kourtney was the baby boy who was the love child of his parents. His family was his anchor, and he cherished the moments spent with them, creating memories that will forever be treasured. Kourtney was not only a son but also a caring brother—a very present presence in the lives of his siblings. He shared in their triumphs and provided comfort in their trials, always ready with a helping hand or a listening ear.

To his sister, brothers and his nieces, Kourtney was a role model and a source of unconditional love.

As a husband, Kourtney's love and devotion to his wife were unwavering. Their love Jones was a testament to their commitment to each other.

Kourtney's friendships were a testament to his genuine love and loyalty. He was a true friend to many, offering a listening ear, a shoulder to lean on, and a hearty laugh during times of joy.

Kourtney was also a cherished nephew, and his presence added a special light to family gatherings. His love and respect for his extended family were evident in the bonds he nurtured.

As a churchgoer, Kourtney was a jovial drummer—a true church boy who found himself and inspiration in his faith.

Kourtney was a true Flintstone—a rock upon which others could rely. His legacy will endure through the love, laughter, and lessons he shared with us all.

As we remember Kourtney, let us also remember the profound impact he had on the lives of those he loved and the many friends he cherished. His memory will live on in the love, faith, and kindness he shared with us all.

In closing, He leaves behind a legacy of love, devotion, and unwavering faith that will continue to inspire us all. A true Hero.

Love,

Mom

Celebrating Unseen Heroes

<u>Honorees</u>

E. Hill De Loney

Dr. E. Hill De Loney's life story is all about making things better for the community. She's made a big impact by working in different roles, from being a leader to organizing Juneteenth events.

She started as the Director of the Flint Odyssey House, Inc., Health Awareness Center, where she made programs to help people with their health. She also led the Community Based Organization Partners (CBOP) and started the Community Based Public Health Initiative (CBPHI).

E. Hill Deloney is really smart too, with master's Degrees in Guidance Counseling and Psychology. She used her knowledge to deal with important issues like teen health, father-son relationships, baby survival, and stopping youth violence.

But she didn't stop there. She also made sure her community celebrated Juneteenth, a day that's important in Black history. She's been doing this for over 50 years!

E. Hill Deloney also worked with the NAACP for a long time and helped the National Association of Black Social Workers (NABSW). She always fought for the rights of people who needed help.

She's been a leader in the American Public Health Association (APHA) too, with important jobs in different groups. There's even an award named after her for groups that do great work with young people.

E. Hill Deloney's mission in life is to make things better for Black families and communities. She's worked really hard to make health better, make things fair, and celebrate culture. Her work will keep making a difference for years to come.

Sybyl Atwood

I was given a special task by Sybyl Atwood, a trailblazer in social work for our community and those without homes. Sybyl Atwood was known for her dedication to our community and her pioneering efforts in supporting homeless individuals. She created a small, pocket-sized resource book, the first of its kind, that included valuable information for everyone in our community, including those who were homeless.

Maicee-Ann Sharon Hill

I am passionate about helping others. I have been a licensed massage therapist and Reiki master for 10 years. In my journey of learning to heal myself and helping others along the way, I decided to return to school to get my master's degree in social work. I plan to work in the mental health field and bring a holistic approach to those needing services. I have had the privilege of spending the last 10 years growing my knowledge and helping people to heal on a physical and spiritual level and now I get to expand my knowledge on helping people to heal on a mental and emotional level as well.

I plan on working from a holistic approach to help people have a complete healing experience. I have knowledge and experience with energy healing techniques such as Reiki which can help people relax their nervous system so they may be able to work through issues that are holding them back. I plan to learn more about techniques such as somatic therapy, internal family systems therapy, substance abuse counseling, and cognitive behavioral therapy.

My passion is to help those struggling with mental health and addiction issues. These issues hit close to home as I, as well as the people I love, have struggled with both of these issues. I want to be able to show others they have the power within themselves to change their lives for the better and give support where it is so desperately needed.

You can email me at Maiceehill22@gmail.com

The Looking Glass Self
By Maicee Ann Sharon Hill

From Trial to Triumph. Examining the social psychology theory of "The Looking-Glass Self" through personal experience and self-discovery: In the realm of social psychology there is an intriguing theory called "The Looking-Glass Self". It examines how humans perceive their self-image. In the "Looking-Glass Self" theory a person's self-image is based on how they perceive others to see them. Your self-worth and self-image become merely an image reflected back to you through the perception of those around you. In my early years of life, I found myself plagued with the downfalls of this concept. From my earliest memories, I felt like an outsider in every group. I can remember being enveloped with a deep sense of loneliness. This led me to a deep depression that only continued to grow as I got older.

In my teen years, I began finding my place within a group of friends in which I started to build my sense of self-image. Akin to Alice falling down the rabbit hole I became fixated on chasing that white rabbit of self-esteem by molding that reflection of myself into what I thought others wanted me to be. Igniting the neurons in my brain to search for the sensation of connection outside of myself. A small spark that turned into a blazing fire. I played with a lot of fire during those years. Since I could never internally stimulate my sense of connection and self-worth. I then turned to substances at 13 to numb the pain of what I could not give myself. Temporarily drowning out the voice of self-doubt telling me I was never good enough. I felt my self-worth was in being accepted by other people.

When we need other people's approval to feel worthy of just being ourselves this leads to pitfalls of depression. Because the acceptance of "you" is based on external resources that need to be replenished.

At 14 my family had to move away from my familiar home and friends due to a job change my father had. I was now supposed to pack my bags and move across the state leaving behind the only version of myself I thought I knew. When we made it to the new place, I was supposed to now call home, I fell into a deep depression. People tend to think depression is simply feeling sad and it's not. It's more of the feeling of being empty. Things that you know are supposed to make you happy and leave you feeling just as empty as before. When you lack the sensation to feel anything at all you can begin to look for ways to feel something, anything, even pain. I began self-harming and I struggled with severe insomnia. Even as I tried to rest, the negative persisting thoughts would never leave me alone.

The combination of all of this led to being prescribed antipsychotic medications which never seemed to help me and only made the negative thoughts worse. Looking back now I see I had no self-image. My self-image was a reflection from behind other people's eyes and when that was gone, I had nothing.

I had no idea how to pick myself up from that. I began searching for self-worth in other relationships. As I got older, I searched for self-worth in romantic relationships. Which pulled me down a toxic and abusive road. I accepted pain and emotional abuse for glimpses of love and affection. I began running into the same problems over and over again with different faces. Different masks the universe wore to try to get me to learn the lesson I was supposed to learn out of all of this. Which brings us to the question, how do we shatter the illusion of the looking-glass self? How do we break the chains we have placed upon our self-image? If we constantly need to feel other people's approval to have a positive self-image of ourselves, how can we ever feel complete?

My road to breaking the concept of this looking-glass self was jagged and winding. It's not a straight road, it comes with many twists and turns. Bringing you back to points you already passed along the way. However, we can create a new path for ourselves. We can embrace the unfamiliar and shatter the illusion we have created in our minds of who we are supposed to be. We don't have to dull our sharp edges to fit into a box labeled "acceptable" by the rest of society. Instead, we can use those sharp edges of uniqueness and self-expression to cut through those chains we have placed upon ourselves. As a quote from the book "The Magic of Awareness" by Anam Thubten and Sharon Roe states, "Good concepts are like gold chains, and bad concepts are like iron chains. They both equally bind you in the end."

The truth is there is no map to the road of self-acceptance. The journey is going to look different for everyone. I can only speak from my own experience of where my winding road has taken me. For me, pain was my biggest teacher. Only through the pain of staying the same did I bring out the will to claw my way through the pain of change. I could no longer allow others to be the source of my own personal power. So, I picked myself up and took a leap of faith into change. I made small changes, like enrolling in massage school which opened the door to learn many new things. Learning about anatomy and physiology helped me understand how the human body worked. I was also introduced to energy healing which helped me understand that I had the power within myself to heal the parts of me that left me feeling so alone.

That was my big awakening to igniting the fire of my own self-power. Instead of the blazing fire of self-destruction that had once ruled the neurons in my brain, I realized the power to love myself and heal myself was within my own hands the whole time. This was the fire of my soul. Instead of needing fuel from outside of myself, this fire was self-sustaining. Instead of bringing me exhaustion and emptiness, it brought passion and desire. I began taking better care of myself. I started eating healthier and exercising regularly. I began meditating and changing my thought patterns. I was finally able to see the subtle beauty in life and within myself. I was starting to understand what the true feeling of peace was. Learning how to connect with my inner world and to stop fighting with the voice inside my head brought love and peace into the temple of my body and mind. With that, I also started on the path of helping others to heal in the same way.

When I first started this work within myself, entering my mind was like entering a room full of funhouse mirrors. There were so many images of myself, all distorted reflections I had created in my psyche. I had to look at each one and see each reflection for the illusion that it was. When you see the distortions for the illusions that they are, the image breaks. It shatters into tiny bits of glass that no longer hold that image in your mind. This is the power you hold within yourself to create your own life. To not let this world hold you captive with its delusions. It can be a very painful process when you begin to face the parts of yourself that you have not wanted to look at.

You can feel like you are breaking inside. This is just the shattering of the illusion coming down. It's the breaking of the looking glass. Allow yourself to shatter, allow yourself to break and crumble, and feel the weight you have been holding over yourself. Breaking is not the end, only the beginning. Once you break you can pick yourself back up again and create whatever image you want. You will become the artist of your own life's masterpiece. Paint with your soul instead of other people's expectations, or even the expectations you have placed upon yourself. Toss those to the side as the pieces you no longer need. Allow yourself to swim in the glory of your reflection, sharp edges, and all.

This work does not have a finish line. That's okay because it is the work of life itself. We constantly change and evolve. Life would be quite boring if we didn't. Always see the beauty in the subtle things.

Allow yourself to be fully present in as many moments as possible. Have a thirst for life and replenish the waters of your soul with self-love and acceptance. Nothing has to be perfect. It is better when it's not. We don't grow in perfection. We need all elements of life to flourish. It's how we handle things that matter. How we construct the vision of our own lives is what we get to take with us when we leave here. We won't take things, profits, or social status with us. We get to leave others with the memories we gave them and bring with us the love we held onto while we were here.

Life is too short to be burdened with the things that do not serve us. Your inner power is too precious to rely on others to replenish it. It's good to feel accepted and loved by others; it is part of the human condition. However, when we cross that line into needing it, we give our power away and become lost. Some people label this as codependency. It's something a lot of people struggle with. Because we are designed by nature to want approval from other people. We all

fall victim to the concept of "The Need to Belong".
Don't let it consume you.

When it becomes a need, a craving, and begins
to make your life unmanageable, it becomes an
addiction. We can heal from addiction in all of its
forms.

I am no stranger to the grips of addiction. I
have had my issues with using substances to cope, and
with using the affection of other people to feel worthy
of just being alive. I have had loved ones who have
struggled with addiction and was lucky enough to
watch them on their path to sobriety. I also worked as a
recovery coach and worked with people on their road
to recovery. I have never been more inspired than
when I had the privilege of sitting in a room full of
people who had experienced traumas that most people
could not even dream of in their worst nightmares.
Who brought themselves out of the darkest moments
of their lives, sitting in a room together with the sole
intention of facing the deepest parts of themselves to

heal and become the best version of themselves they can be.

Any addiction, whether it is a substance addiction or a behavioral addiction, stems from the same process in the brain. Addiction itself comes from not being at peace within your mind and body, from a lack of connection to yourself and the world around you. Addiction is a complex problem that can take on many different forms. However, it all branches out from the same root. If we stop judging how the addiction is presenting itself and start addressing the root cause, we will have a much better chance of erasing the problem altogether. We as a society don't want to look at addiction in the face. We want to treat it as a personal problem rather than a societal one. We continually ostracize people struggling with addiction which continues the cycle of addiction.

The same areas in the brain that are activated during physical pain are also activated when people feel rejection. It has been shown in studies that taking a pain reducer can also soothe pain from social rejection. Imagine how hard it is to break the cycle when the whole of society is constantly rejecting those who are in the most need of understanding and connection. It does not matter if you are addicted to cocaine or shopping. To society, one may look better than the other but what is taking place in the brain is the same. Changing how we label addiction and look at addiction can help us heal the roots of addiction. We must not only break down the illusions we have constructed about ourselves but about others as well. Once you start breaking down your illusions you will start to see the illusions society has placed upon us as well.

My own personal struggles and the journey of my own healing have now taken me down the path of beginning my career in social work. I took that step to go back to school so I could help other people in a new way. To be able to use my own story to help be a voice for others. I'm excited about this road and to be able to bring all the knowledge I already have into this field where it is so desperately needed. We need to bring our light into the darkest parts of humanity to heal as a community. That journey starts with self-healing. We can help soften suffering with love, compassion, and understanding but first, we must give that to ourselves.

I am somebody who has taken that step and put my healing into my own hands. Where it should have been all along, it's okay to be afraid of the unknown. Don't let that fear become the roadblock to your own journey. Find ways to allow yourself to process and heal. One of the ways I allow energy to move through me is by writing. Writing this chapter for this book has been a healing process for me. I have always written poetry and had a journal to write my thoughts into. Find things that help you move the energy of your mind. Otherwise, it can become too easy to stay stuck there. I will end this chapter with a short poem I wrote some years ago on the winding road that has been my own journey. The mind is a beautiful thing. It does not have to become your prison. Let the illusion of the looking-glass self-break and you will find your way home.

Labyrinth labyrinth make me whole
Show me the way back to my own soul
My mind is shattered my body is broken
The only thing left is for my soul to be open
Labyrinth labyrinth set me free
Remind me who it is I'm supposed to be
Within your walls, you hold the key
To all the things I can not see
Help me shatter the illusion in the looking glass
Break free from all the pain of the present and
the past
Pull down the veil and reveal the truth
to me at last
Take off the mask, light the way on
my path unload upon me your mysteries
so vast
A glimmer of hope is all I have of you to ask
Cut right through the ties that bind
Unweave the web you so tightly wind
Labyrinth labyrinth give me time
To make it out of this maze that is
My own mind

Monsiou Dimerson, MSW

Ever since I can remember, I've had a strong sense of caring for others and wanting to help. Being understanding, strong, kind, and empathetic has always been a big part of who I am. These qualities have led me to build close relationships with the people I've met along the way. Life has thrown its fair share of trials at me, but I've faced them all with a heart full of love, a spirit of triumph, and the belief that I could turn tough times into something sweet, just like making lemonade from sour lemons.

Social work core values and principles I practice and believe build rapport and growth mindsets for clients served are integrity, competence, dignity and worth, the importance of human relationships, environmental care, professional behavior, and simply being my authentic self. As a social worker, I'm cautious while providing goals. My clients deserve achievable goals while maintaining their livelihoods. No one should be given tools without guidance on how to begin and maintain them. I aim to help them learn how to regulate and understand how their mind works by understanding patterns, history, and habits. Furthermore, I need to provide resources for clients when applicable and build a network of support within their community for a greater chance of success.

I am drawn to and passionate about children and the homeless population and am currently in the process of becoming a life coach. I am committed to enduring new information to understand the needs and barriers of individuals, communities, and educational systems. Everyone deserves a chance at a great life, but not many people know they have choices to create one. We all deserve a hero, not to be saved but to help remember our importance and rights to happiness, success, and love.

Let's connect, I enjoy hearing stories, creating new perspectives, and planning for new adventures. Let's do it together, one step at a time.

Linktree: https://linktr.ee/monidmsw

Direction Forward

By Monsiou Dimerson, MSW

Social work was a given, I always knew I was designed to help others. Since I was a little girl I had gifts specially given for people like me who could handle them while pushing through unexpected life events. Everything came naturally when I began my journey as a social worker, I made connections authentically and my healing began to grow.

My vision of uplifting others, one person at a time, shaped my perspective and interest in social work. At the beginning of my college journey, I wasn't sure what I wanted to major in, but I knew I was a helper. Over time my vision became much clearer. Social work supported the following areas of my interest: empowering others, education, and supporting communities in multiple settings. I had the pleasure of assisting in nursing homes, hospitals, assisted living facilities, and school settings since becoming a social worker.

Listening to my classmates' different life events and challenges shaped my perspective on social work as well. Classmates would tell me stories of being homeless, their childhood trauma, abuse, challenges with family, and survival stories like my own. There were many inspirational people that I connected with while in school. Everyone's unique story reassured me that it's possible to overcome trials in life and continue college. Pursuing my career in social work gave me knowledge that no one was able to take away. With social work, I can spread light, love, my voice, and knowledge. I began to notice my personal growth and healing journey. Growth didn't come easy; I am still growing with new challenges to overcome daily. As humans, we have battles in our minds that can either lead us to victory or destruction. While in college I learned about emotional intelligence and how effective it was while connecting with others. With emotional intelligence, we have a better chance of achieving goals and improving our quality of life. Living each day without the feeling of worry, fear, loneliness, and doubt became easier. However, once one accomplishment is made, we have to remember to continue the journey and begin climbing the next mountain top.

No one should have to suffer; everyone should have support and resources to thrive and reach their fullest potential. There may come a time in our lives when we question how we can make a difference. Social work was my answer to being involved in making a difference.

The reflection of my life's trials and triumphs kept me motivated daily to study social work and contribute to empowering transformations. Growing up wasn't easy, there were many challenges such as hearing and the aftermath of a fatal shooting outside

my window, my mother going to prison, my brother
unexpectedly dying with little to no explanation on the
cause, my second love's fatal death in a car accident,
close encounters with me dying from being in the same
area during a shooting, experiencing an abusive
relationship, my cousin dying a week after overdosing
in my apartment, and experiencing poverty, and
homelessness. There were many more challenging
situations I overcame, but I often remind myself that
social work creates an additional layer of strength, and
with that strength comes choices allowing me to open
the doors for more opportunities, growth, connection,
healing, and resilience.

College was my outlet for the start of a new
beginning. I stayed up late many nights working on
assignments, I remember wanting to give up, but I kept
going tired, frustrated, and confused. There were many
goals I made plans for and dedicated my time to. I
worked full-time while working on college courses and

completing internships as a single mother of two girls.
Many people doubted me, and others supported and
believed in me. There was no time to hang out with
friends. Many of my friendships ended by choosing to
make a difference in me and my daughter's lives. I
began outgrowing my circle of friends and started
making new friends. While in college I began to learn
more about my emotions and life. I connected with
many professors on a deeper level to understand my
worth and complete my work to the best of my ability
each year and never gave up. I was at the finish line; it
didn't matter if no one else believed in me because I
believed in myself. I have no regrets, but if I could
rewind time, I would have enjoyed the journey while
studying social work in college. I let current
circumstances interrupt my joy daily, I didn't express
gratitude and allow myself grace when it came to life
challenges and mistakes I've made as a younger adult.

Now that I am working in the field, I am experiencing different levels of challenges. Remembering to create boundaries can be challenging. As humans, we want to do more than we are required to do, especially while helping others in social work. There have been many days where I experienced burnout. I would forget to take time and reflect on the density of my workload. I learned to eliminate what was less important and or unnecessary for the moment and started forming lists starting from the most important need daily. Doing this allowed me to brainstorm ideas, take time with solutions, and gather the support needed to effectively serve clients.

There are some cases when I learned to include my gifts of discernment or what others may call intuition while providing services. I believe it is important to challenge your clients. Understanding their past is important but getting deep in the core of their unwanted thoughts and actions is important to work on ways to create change. There's a natural urge to want everyone I connect with to understand who they are authentically and recognize the greatness they provide to the world.

Many people believe themselves to be what they endured from their circumstances. An understanding of oneself is a must; it provides an opportunity for individuals to dive into the natural state of being and the importance of life.

Children are pure and innocent. Many of the children that I worked with over the years reacted to their unwanted circumstances with anger, sadness, dissociation, and/ or self-harm. Children need to know that they are special and should have genuine support and compassion from their family and friends. Support and compassion are not always provided to the students I work with. Many families are broken with no communication and sense of direction. Many people are afraid and lack trust while connecting with mental health professionals due to systems failing them creating additional layers of trauma.

I began seeing the difference I made as a social worker working in different communities and collaborating with other professionals. Many children that I connected with had difficulties while in school due to their trauma, mental illness, and/ or disabilities. The students begin to lack confidence and empowerment due to their needs impeding their education. There were many moments of uncertainty and situations that I never experienced. The moments of doubt led to me questioning whether I was effective in the needs of my clients. I had to utilize my characteristics of empathy, compassion, and resilience and put myself in the place of each client. I then created plans for them based on their needs. Many moments were impactful while connecting with communities and clients. The most memorable moments thus far were in the school settings a year after the coronavirus outbreak. Many students and families were impacted. Education took a turn in addition to the rise of mental illness, homelessness, divorces, and death. I spent a lot of time connecting with communities and programs that I believed would support the students outside the school setting. During this time many of us professionals were experiencing the same situations as the students were, which led to gaps of miscommunication in the school settings.

The experience I encountered with students and families post-pandemic reinforced my dedication to the social work profession by learning and discovering my blueprint. Emotional intelligence wasn't enough, my blueprint included understanding what I represented, what was missing in my life, loving myself more, and remembering to enjoy the journey while continuing to build meaningful connections with people who elevated me.

These qualities and values of my blueprint gave me a brief understanding of who I am and why my work is valuable to those that I serve. As a social worker, I like to understand my clients on a personal level to connect with them and provide applicable tools. Reminding my clients that healing is an everlasting journey that we must take time to enjoy is a very important step for me while supporting my clients. There should always be excitement in growth, healing is not just a reminder of pain, it's a reminder of survival and resilience.

Self-discovery is one of the best gifts we can give to ourselves. We must set boundaries for those that are unworthy of our time and space. We have to continue to understand our calling and work on our goals consistently to see results. We don't have time to wait for things to get better, do it amid chaos and discomfort. We have to believe in every move we make and choose wisely. No one owes us anything, we owe happiness to ourselves. I understand that I can't feel bad for myself due to my circumstances. I stopped having expectations of other people and life itself and started believing in my abilities to overcome obstacles no matter what came my way. Letting go of the unwanted person I became due to my trauma was challenging.

I took advantage of the opportunity to connect with people who taught and guided me to become the best version of myself. With my true self, I begin eliminating habits and creating new ones. I became my own hero every day and said yes to myself, yes to winning, and yes to new opportunities. I want to encourage you to become your hero every day, anything is possible if you truly believe.

Shanta Smith, MS, BSW, CSS

In the remarkable journey of Shanta Natre Smith, known to many as "The Eagle," we find the story of a true blessing. Shanta is a multi-talented artist, writer, producer, clothing designer, and engineer. He seamlessly blends soul, hip-hop, street culture, and spirituality into his music, crafting a one-of-a-kind sound he lovingly refers to as "soul food." With an extraordinary ability to infuse his heart and soul into his records, Shanta reaches the very core of his listeners. His powerful presence on stage and his gift for ministry leaves an indescribable feeling on all who have had the privilege of experiencing his ministry.

Shanta's musical odyssey began at the tender age of 12 while he was in foster care. During those challenging times, he honed his craft by pouring his pain, emotions, and experiences into his music. Rather than dwelling on the hardships he faced, Shanta used his music as a beacon of hope. His unique style draws inspiration from a diverse range of artists, including the iconic Michael Jackson (with whom he shares a birthdate), Al Green, 2Pac, and John P. Kee, among others. Shanta's focus isn't necessarily on adversity; he's on a remarkable journey of resilience to triumph. Despite dropping out of school multiple times and enduring a traumatic past, he rose above the ashes as a source of inspiration for those still struggling with mental and physical bondage.

Shanta's educational pursuits further demonstrate his commitment to overcoming adversity. He earned a bachelor's degree in social work and a master's degree in criminal justice, a testament to his dedication to making a positive impact on the lives of others. Now, his mission is to reach back into the ashes and share God's message with believers and non-believers alike, reigniting the flame of faith within God's people.

Shanta embarked on his professional career as part of the group Bloodlines A.D., alongside his older twin brothers, Tamiekco and Damiekco. Their journey took flight with the release of their maxi single "Fallen Angels" in 1999, during which they shared the stage with industry luminaries like Busta Rhymes, Dayton Family, and MC Breed. However, life has a way of changing our course, and Shanta's path was no exception.

Turning away from the streets, Shanta launched. his first solo gospel album, "Emergency," released in August 2019. Midway through this transformative project, Shanta joined forces with the talented singer and rapper Antoine Brown to form "The Eagle and the Lion." Together, they embarked on regional tours to promote Shanta's "Emergency" album, while also collaborating on their duo project, "Detox," releasing its single in October 2019. Their performances graced venues such as the Civic Center, The Horizon Event Center in Saginaw, the Dort Federal Event Center, local events, and many local churches.

Linktree: https://linktr.ee/shanta_smith

Madness to Miracles, Living Unleashed, By Shanta Smith, MS, BSW, CSS

Before I found freedom and peace of mind I first had to journey through the valley of the shadow of death and faced what looked like at the time an army of giants. Growing up in Flint Michigan, I had a troubled childhood. In my neighborhood, poverty was the norm but due to my mother and father's drug and alcohol addiction, my family fell even below that line. As a child not understanding the power, hold, and influence that drugs had over my parents' choices, I struggled with low self-esteem and depression from neglect and abuse. This led me to the streets to meet my needs and eventually to start using myself to manage and cope with the trauma and feelings of abandonment. In the valley experience, it was hard to see the road to freedom and the path that God was paving for me.

I had two older brothers who were twins who chose a different path. They were in college at Ferris State University. One Christmas day I was kicked out of my cousin's house and my brothers came to pick me up and introduced me to another way of living. I was not ready at the time because my mind was still afflicted with a poverty mentality, and they eventually said I had to leave there also. Back to the streets of Flint I went but it was different, I had been exposed to possibilities that left a craving in my mouth for something more. It was enough to get me to graduate high school but not enough to fight back the demons that plagued my heart and mind.

Feeling alone in a world of chaos that I created filled with trauma and violence that comes with the street life, my addiction grew. Unable to see a way out of a way of living I hated, I decided I had had enough. I attempted suicide and by the grace of God and My guardian angel who today is my wife I survived.

Being In the Hospital on the mental health floor was my turning point, it was on floor 7 at Hurley hospital where I decided to have a conversation with God. I made a promise since he spared my life, I was going to try it His way. Finally, I began to confront my giants, the trauma, fear, anger, abandonment, and resentments, and slowly began to heal. I enrolled in college and after taking a course in sociology my purpose was clear and my past finally made sense.

Barriers/Giants continued to present themselves to try and discourage me and knock me off course, for example. The social work board and even my college counselor strongly encouraged me to change my major due to my criminal history and denied me entrance into the program. Take note; The enemy always tries to remind us of our mistakes and our past, it is his job to accuse us and disqualify us, so we give up and never receive our reward. With a strong understanding of grace and who I was in Christ, my path was clear, and I refused to accept that as an answer and wrote a letter explaining my history, who I was then, my thinking, and more importantly who I was now. They accepted me into the program and explained that I would have a near impossible path ahead. They explained that employers would not hire me, and I would be lucky to even get an internship.

Every step in my journey was faced with barriers. After graduating with my bachelor's in social work, I applied for many social work positions. I was an excellent interviewer, so all of my interviews were successful, however, once a background search was completed, it was like a bad song stuck on repeat. (We are sorry but unfortunately due to your record). I heard this over and over again. At this point in my life, I was married and had just given birth to my first child and could not find employment. Bills were piled up and I no longer participated in my old extracurricular activities. Eventually the fire Marshall showed up at our door explaining that we had 3 days before they executed the eviction.

I was in Limbo, it felt like I was punched in the gut by Mike Tyson and smacked in the face by God. I was doing everything right, going to church, being faithful, paying my tithes, and giving my offerings. All of a sudden, the old me started to speak to me. Get your gun to hit a lick, with your skill set you'll be good by Monday. Standing in the front of my apartment complex with my pistol in hand looking over my shoulder through the white window blinds of my patio door; I could see my baby playing in her pack-and-play and my wife sitting oblivious of the choice I was getting ready to make.

It was 8:30 pm and I was waiting for the sun to go down. I began crying and talking to myself, the old me who was known as (Thug Chemist), you have been good for over 5 years, you have come too far to turn back. Chemist replied, you are a man. You have to take

care of your family and you don't have anyone to call.
He was right, I began crying even harder and I
remembered one person that I had not yet given a call.
I looked to the grayish darkening sky and began to pray
and speak with God my father. I reminded him of his
word and the promises that are in it. I heard a voice in
my spirit, it was not audible, but I could hear it clearly.
It said, just go in the house. I remember shaking my
head indicating that was not a solution, not even an
option. I heard the voice again and again. I cried one
last time and said OK.

With no answer, no solution, and no moves to
make, I walked in, put my gun back in place, and sat
quietly on the couch for at the most 2 minutes. The
phone rang and my wife answered. She said it's for you.
I said as quietly as I could trying to hide my thoughts
and feelings, I don't want to talk to anybody right now.
She relayed the message, then turned to me and said,
"It's Ms. Jacqueline." My response was I don't know

any Ms. Jacquelines. She said she would like to speak with you.

Frustrated with almost no life in my body I grabbed the phone and said hello. The voice on the other end of the line was high spirited and she said hello My Name is Ms. Jacqueline from Flint Odyssey House you dropped your resume off a few months back and we want to know if you are interested in a Job.

I have been working at Flint Odyssey House for over 16 years now. I started as a youth counselor, shortly moved into adult counseling, was promoted to coordinator, and eventually director of Co-ed services where I supervised clinical staff.

What I thought were curses were training and preparation to help others shrink their giants to ant size. Having experienced the gut-wrenching blow of addiction and poverty firsthand and the effects it has on youth, family, community, and the world, I felt a deep connection to others going through their valley experience. I share my story, not only to heal myself but also to inspire others to seek help and never lose hope no matter how big the problems appear. God transformed what appeared to be a throwaway, a write-off, a problem child into a grown man, a husband, a father, and a hope dealer.

Being a social worker in this field, I have been a part of the change process of so many men women, and children. Seeing them come into the program looking like death is waiting on their next breath to transform into positive role models within their community. Let me tell you how funny God is sometimes. When I was 16 years old, I was somewhere my mother told me not to go and ended up getting attacked by a gang and was blinded. The doctors said it's a 90% chance that it would be permanent. Just recently I was counseling a woman and learned that she was the mother of the lifelong enemy that took my sight. I know right, "crazy". I learned that when you have a heart for people and God, forgiveness and humility is easy.

I have been blessed with many gifts and talents and today I use them as vehicles to reach, inspire, motivate, and provoke change.

Music is one of my gifts and the way I minister to others. I share my experiences and my journey. With an understanding now that all things are possible according to his will, designed and built a recording studio. I put my heart and soul into crafting music that resonates with the young or old, rich, or poor, saved, or unsaved folks who are faced with the challenges that life brings. Songs such as "Keys to the Kingdom" and "Love for You" have become anthems and are therapeutic to those who are lost or need motivation to face adversity. As my music continues to gain attention, I pray that I can have an even greater impact on the lives it comes across.

Drawing inspiration from my past experience, spiritual relationship, and professional clinical knowledge, I launched a clothing line that sends a powerful message to the mind, aimed at encouraging individuals not to let barriers or life challenges cage them nor define who they are or what they are to become. "Unleashed".

The Unleashed clothing line serves as a reminder that no matter what situation you are born into, what your economic situation is, or how tough life can get, it is possible to rise above any circumstance and walk in purpose with passion to reach your destiny. Through my Clinical practice, music, and clothing line, I am on a mission to role model, inspire, educate, and empower others to break free from the mental chains of self-doubt, dependency, and societal expectations.

I hope that the fruits of my labor will become a symbol of hope and transformation in my community and expand around the globe.

Let my story be a living testimony of the power of God, that through faith and determination, you can overcome any obstacles, and defeat any giant regardless of what it looks like. I have traveled through mountains high and valleys low, hell sleet, and snow to stand before you as a successful 3 time felon, high school dropout with a bachelor's degree in social work and a master's in criminal justice, married with children living in a 5-bedroom house fully paid for with no loans, business owner with no loans. I only had to look to the father who reminded me who I was and more importantly who I was not. I am not my mistakes, I am not a hoodlum, I am not a whore monger, I am not poor, I am not forgotten but I am blessed.

As a clinical social worker, I understand that traumatic events in our childhood and how we perceive them affect how we act and respond as adults. But God takes our past hurt and pain and transforms it into a testimony of healing. It is never too late to pivot, to change the direction of your life and anything is possible according to his will. Remember you are custom built with everything you need on the inside of you, tap into the gifts and talents that God has installed in you and unleash them. What you don't have he will provide. He has given you the keys to the kingdom. You are his sons and daughters; it is time to live like it.

Katie Colding, LCSW

I am a compassionate and devoted social worker with a deep commitment to private mental health practice and medical social work practices. With only four years of experience in the field, I have had the privilege of serving multiple populations including hospice, elementary students as a school social worker, acute medically impaired individuals, and intensive outpatient clients.

I believe in meeting each person where they are at. Empathy, respect, and confidentiality are the foundations of my practice. I strive to help my clients achieve their goals and navigate life's challenges. My personal goal is to provide a safe space for each individual to comfortably express themselves and be vulnerable with their current stressors and emotions.

I specialize in working with people experiencing grief and loss. I understand the pain and emptiness that comes with such an event and am compassionate about sitting with each client in their experience.

I am always eager to connect with individuals and organizations who share a commitment to mental health practice.

Feel free to reach out to me at katie@mixednutscounseling.com or find me on Psychology Today for a consultation or initiation of individual counseling.

Follow Me: Website
www.mixednutscounseling.com

Totally Stumped: Turning Pain into Passion

By Katie Colding, LCSW

While some people show hesitation about a social worker being involved in their affairs, others welcome the thought of a resourceful helpmate. Some expect us to provide the solution to any demand, while others look to us for guidance, finding comfort in our ability to sort through the tangled web of their thoughts or situations. Some of the individuals we encounter just need a safe space to sit with their most vulnerable selves and feel understood. Then some sing our praises while others avoid our attempts to hold them accountable for the things, they have asked us to help them change. No matter which side the coin lands on, the truth is we endure a lot as social workers.

Being a social worker requires mental fortitude and learning to refine our balance of life. I don't know one professional in this field who can say they have not had to improve themselves in the process of becoming a great clinician.

We are human, and although we are looked upon for guidance and direction, we too must overcome the uncontrollable obstacles life throws our way. I had to overcome a major hurdle right in the middle of getting my degree. I am happy to say I am now on the other side, but in the midst of it, I was yearning for internal peace.

To provide a little background about my trials, let me give you the short version. I grew up in a small town where everybody knows everybody and their business. When I was 22 months old, I was in a lawn mower accident where I lost half of my right foot and the big toe on the left. I spent most of my childhood feeling like "the different girl." I can admit no one was outright mean to my face, but I wore that insecurity loudly. I didn't realize it until I was older, but I responded to that insecurity by seeking validation from others. In my mind, I needed to be accepted because I was different and the best way to do that was by showing kindness and helping people. In turn, people knew they could depend on me, and I was often told they did not feel judged by me. I was always the friend that everyone came to when they needed someone to listen or rely on.

Let's fast forward to college. I was one week into my senior year when my father passed away. Life has now changed forever. I was 20 years old and barely had a grip on life. My priorities instantly changed, and anxiety and depression rushed in like a raging river. I went through every emotion. It was the hardest thing I had experienced in life so far. I finally gave in to my family's request to go to therapy, and that experience changed my life. I finished therapy with the mindset of wanting to help other people be able to feel better or just feel again, the way my therapist did for me. I graduated with an unrelated bachelor's degree later that year.

I took some time to process my pain and do some soul-searching. I reestablished my relationship with God and had a dear friend who encouraged me to go back to church. I took a couple of years off from school, but I always knew I would get another degree. I wasn't sure of my direction at the time and began researching different avenues. I had a lot of options, but nothing felt right. Then I had someone tell me they drove by Saint Leo University and thought of me. At the time I didn't think anything of it, but a year later I remembered that and decided to look at their programs. There it was... the Master of Social Work program. As soon as I read the summary, I knew it was for me. It was everything I was looking for and more. I immediately began working toward my enrollment.

In 2017 I was accepted into the fall semester and began my journey. I honestly had no idea what I was going to do with my degree. Social work is a very broad field, and I just knew I wanted to help people feel better. The first semester was tough, but that's to be expected. The second semester was better, and I was excited to start an internship. School was going great, but in my personal life, anxiety was starting to build as I began to have pains and issues with my right ankle and nub foot. As I addressed it medically, I was encouraged to think about having the rest of my foot amputated and taken to a below-knee amputation. It wasn't the first time this suggestion was brought to me, but this time the idea seemed more impending than before.

As the pains grew, I started having consultations with surgeons and talking with my prosthetist more. My anxiety soared to new levels while trying to figure out how to make such a decision. I had just started my first internship when this ordeal became a reality. It was an internship I was excited about, but I often found myself drifting off into thought and not being as present as I would have liked. I was able to get through most of my day remaining mindful of the tasks at hand, but as soon as I got home my reality was focused on, "Am I about to have another amputation?" I found ways to distract myself, but in all honesty, the anxiety was crippling. I can remember praying a lot and asking God to tell me what to do, but deep down I knew it had to be done.

My mom had a hard time coming to terms with the situation. She was not in favor of me going through with further amputation. I could tell it was eating at her. She went to most of the consultations with me and tried to educate herself on the process. Then one day in May of 2018, my mom and I met with a surgeon at the same hospital where I was an intern. He answered all our questions and helped me feel confident in him. I found myself in his office with the scheduling receptionist and suddenly it all became very real. The lady stepped out of the office for a moment and tears flooded my face as I asked my mom if I was doing the right thing. Tearfully, she encouraged me and affirmed her support for me no matter what I did. I left the surgeon's office that day knowing the rest of my life was about to change.

I set the surgery date for August 17th. This was an intentional decision because it was my only week off from school. We had a short break from the summer semester into the fall. I knew I would want to take the days before the surgery to prepare and pamper myself. The time leading up to surgery was my continued pursuit of doing well in my master's program and trying to work as much as I could. I ended up needing FMLA as the physical pain worsened. There was a weekend for school that we all had to meet on campus, and I can remember needing to be pushed in a wheelchair. I was genuinely surprised that my discomfort became anguish in such a short time. I spent so many years being active and an athlete. I did things I was told I would never do. I began to question how I got to this point. How could I have prevented this? My anxiety was still very present but decided to invite its friend Grief along for the ride too.

The day before my surgery I got a massage. I was trying my best to find peace and relaxation. I had family come into town and we went to dinner that night. I was asked a lot of questions and I know there was a conversation I don't remember. All I wanted to do was be home and left alone. I wanted to spend time with God because I knew I could find rest in Him. Suddenly, it's the morning of my surgery and my mom is driving me to the hospital. It was very early, but I was greeted by more family than I expected and can remember feeling so loved. I appreciated their support more than I was able to express. I was so thankful for my family's presence and to know the team I was interning with was working that day too.

I asked to be checked in right away before I had too much time to think about what was about to happen. I was taken to pre-op and was allowed to have two people back with me. My family took turns coming in to wish me well. I asked the nurse to be put under sooner than later because I did not want to panic. I don't remember her name, but I remember her being very compassionate and helping me feel confident. Next thing I know I am waking up and can see that I am being wheeled into a hospital room. The team I was interning with had a banner and care basket waiting for me. My family was also gathered around. I was coming off anesthesia and while I don't remember much of what was said, I do remember asking my nurse what they did with my foot they cut off. He told me they gave it to him, and he was going to make a lamp out of it and the toes would be the on/off switch. I laughed hysterically but told him I knew he was lying because I didn't have any toes on that foot. Everyone had a good laugh.

That first night after surgery was horrible. I remember waking up in the middle of the night screaming from pain. The weeks following were also difficult and filled with managing the spasms of pain. I learned that while anesthesia provides great sleep, the effects afterward are not desirable. My emotions were all over the place and it didn't take much to cry. I was anxious to do anything that could potentially prolong the healing process. I had a lot of help during the weeks following but accepting that help was not easy. I suddenly went from an extremely independent lady to completely dependent.

Continuing with school was a little more challenging, but with accommodations and very understanding professors, I made it through. A year later I graduated with my cohort and received my Master of Social Work degree. The time between surgery and graduation was arduous. I had another internship, projects, multiple papers, and exams, all while going to physical therapy, healing from surgery physically and mentally, adjusting to a new way of life, and being fitted for a new prosthetic. The adjustment was the hardest part. I was often frustrated with an overwhelming amount of change.

Five years later, I can say that I wouldn't want it any other way. This is part of who I am, and God continues to reveal my purpose in this experience. I was able to turn my pain into my passion. I am helping others like I aspired to do. As a Licensed Clinical Social Worker, I specialize in grief/loss, anxiety, building self-esteem, and depression. I can walk beside my clients on their journey because I know what it feels like. I understand the immeasurable pain of losing someone you love, losing yourself, disabling medical issues, crippling anxiety, and depression that tells us we aren't good enough. I know the struggle that comes with clawing your way out of the pit of disparity. I've climbed the ladder that is healing and discovering peace. I have overcome! All I want is to help others overcome too.

Dr. Kent Key (MPH, PhD)

Dr. Kent Key (MPH, PhD), a resident deeply connected to his community, has turned challenges into triumphs. He is a Professor at Michigan State University, College of Human Medicine, in the Charles Stewart Mott Department of Public Health. Dr. Key is a Health Disparities Researcher utilizing community engaged research approaches to elevate community voice to create community driven solutions to health. He is a health equity scholar, focused on the dismantling of systemic inequities that create unfair outcomes for marginalized communities. Dr. Key ensures that the community has a voice in health decisions, research, policy, and advocacy. He is a national expert in the field of public health. He is a past Chair of the Community Based Public Health Caucus of the American Public Health Association, and 2016 Fellow of the Robert Wood Johnson Foundation, Culture of Health Leaders Program.

One of his biggest achievements is creating the Flint Public Health Youth Academy. A youth empowerment program that gives hope to urban youth by introducing them to medicine, public health, and research, and shows them how to use these careers to advance social justice. Dr. Key is committed to giving Flint youth the opportunity to thrive and become transformative agents of change post the onset of the Flint Water Crisis is his goal. He uses science, music, pop culture, and technology to advance the next generation of public health professionals.

Dr. Key doesn't just work in research; called to the ministry at the age of 12 and ordained at 15, he travels across the country teaching, facilitating, and ministering in word and song. His dedication to his community and his role as a minister is a testament to his perspective that ministry isn't "real ministry" unless you take it out of the four corners of the church. In addition, he serves in county government as a commissioner and the 2023 Chair of the Genesee County Diversity, Equity, and Inclusion Commission. His purpose in both his secular career and his ministry are connected.

Dr. Key's life is a shining example of how one person can make a difference. His saying, "You have not lived until you have done something good for someone who cannot repay," reminds us of the importance of helping others in every way possible.

My Beginning: My Pain, My Trauma
By Dr. Kent Key, Ph.D., M.P.H

As an African American male, I have witnessed the struggles and plight of the urban city, institutional, structural, and systemic racism, and the hustle and bustle of surviving America. I was born and raised in Flint, MI. At one time, Flint was the number one city in the country for household income per capita.

The impact that the automotive industry via General Motors had on Flint catapulted the city to become a leading model in income and finance, education, and other sectors. My introduction to Flint began with parents who had just graduated high school and were learning what it meant to become adults. My mother went to a trade school and earned a license in cosmetology. She later became a business owner and opened a beauty salon. My father chose a different route. He did not want to work for General Motors or any other business. He wanted to be his own boss, and thus, street life was his choice.

At the age of 13, my father was murdered in Flint. The death of my father was the first major mental, cultural, and spiritual pain in my life. As you can imagine, losing my father at the time when I was trying to come to grips with my own identity as a man, especially a black man in America, and finding my sense of purpose was difficult. I struggled in many areas of identity, affirmation, and manifestation of purpose. This was similar to the scene in The Lion King when Simba felt lost and at the water pond searching for his identity after Mufasa was killed. I searched for self, and that process allowed me to transition from pain to purpose.

My Village

As I matured, I realized that I was as strong as the village that supported me. My village was my lifeline. In addition to my mother who worked day and night to send me to private school and to ensure I was in other enrichment activities; my grandparents, other relatives, and mentors provided me with the strength, wisdom, resources, and networks that helped me as I journeyed on my path to purpose. Like many teens and young adults, I made foolish mistakes and did not always listen to the counsel of my elders and the wisdom they had to offer. However, my village stood firm and steadfast with me.

My mentors provided a level of incubation and safety that kept me on the right path. I've had many mentors. Some spiritual, some cultural, some intellectual, and some standing in the gap as a big brother or big sister. As an only child, that mentorship was very important. It was through my mentors that I learned that people who looked like me were the innovators of society. The ancient Africans created mathematics, science, engineering, civics, and government. That was not taught to me in the public school system or private school. Like many African American children, in America, our history is presented as if slavery was our beginning. My mentors taught me that people who looked like me taught the Greeks, the Romans, and other European nations in the first libraries and centers of learning in Africa. This was critically important mentally, culturally, and spiritually for me. The revelation of this truth unlocked the intellectual DNA and capacity that already flowed through my body from the time I was born. This also impacted how I saw myself and guided the way I would contribute to broader society. It inspired me to start the Flint Public Health Youth Academy.

My hope and intent were to create programming that would introduce urban youth, black, brown, and others into the field of public health medicine and research. This scientific program would ensure that youth knew their cultural identity and the rich intellectual capacity and innovation that flowed through their DNA. My mentors mentored me well and now I am mentoring and passing that knowledge to upcoming generations.

Ironically, all mentors are not cliché role models, yet they are equally effective. Not all mentors are teachers, counselors, or coaches. Some of my mentors have been the folk on the street. The drug dealer, the drug addict, and the hustle. Some were related to me, and some were not. These mentors modeled for me "what not to do, "and if they thought I was considering taking the wrong route, they would rebuke me and school me regarding their life's choices. One person, in particular, told me I didn't want to live a life where I would have to constantly look over my shoulder watching for enemies, the police or even being sold out by close friends. He explained the amount of stress and anxiety that was created. He told me that I had too much potential and purpose to achieve. This taught me that my village came in many forms and included "all people" who saw the potential, purpose, and plan that God had for my life, even when I didn't see it. My village protected me from harm, danger, and things that would hurt me. Not only did they protect me from external forces, but they also protected me from my insecurities, my thoughts, and my curiosities.

My Spirituality

I would ascribe my spiritual foundation to my mother's side of the family which would include my mom, maternal grandmother, and my aunt. I basically was born and raised in church and ministry was all I knew. Part of my spiritual evolution was connected to music. My grandmother was the Minister of Music and lead musician at our church from the time I was a baby until my 20s. It was her gifts and talents that she poured into me that led me to become heavily involved in music and ministry. I traveled the country ministering and singing professionally, recording albums with groups and choirs. My mother would purchase children's Bible storybooks and have me read them all the time. My aunt would take her daughter and me to revivals and services that would include Grammy award-winning gospel artists and choirs. This was the foundation that anchored me, and more importantly, created curiosity in me regarding my purpose and my destiny. At the age of 14, I preached my first sermon and was licensed as a minister.

By age 16, I was ordained. Throughout this process, music and worship were constant, and the prophetic was unlocked. Amid all of this, I still struggled with the absence of my father, and the unanswered questions surrounding his death. My paternal grandfather was a dedicated Deacon at his church. His example taught me what dedication and faithfulness was like. He also taught me my word was my bond. He would often say "Real men keep their word." This truth helped to form how I would carry myself when engaging with others. It greatly impacted my character and how I presented myself to the world. Twenty years after losing my father, my maternal grandmother passed away. I was now in my early 20s and felt as if my breath had been knocked out of my body. The impact of this loss shook me to my core. I went into depression and wasn't even aware of it. Things I would love to do such as going to concerts and hanging around friends, I no longer had a desire for and would rather be alone. Now keep in mind, throughout this whole time I have now graduated high school and I'm in college. I'm on the Dean's list, excelling in my academics and doing quite well. I was dealing with functional depression. I was able to function and perform at high levels while still being depressed. My ministry continued throughout this time. I continued to travel the country ministering in both word and song seeing so many people receive their blessings, deliverance, and miracles; yet I would feel empty on the inside. I remember one time asking God, how you can use me to pour life into so many, and yet I feel empty. Then one day after hearing a sermon and spending a weekend in worship the answer came to me clear as day.

The pain that you go through is not for you but is to prepare you to minister to someone else.

Introduction to Public Health

In my early collegiate years, I pursued a degree in engineering because I was good at math and science. I think I enjoyed math because it could not be manipulated with revisionist thoughts and ideologies like we see in the history books. Two plus two would always equal four no matter who was calculating it. I found safety in that, unlike in history, when we were taught that Christopher Columbus discovered America knowing very well people were here when he arrived. So, I pursued a degree in engineering at General Motors Institute now known as Kettering University. In my sophomore year, I joined the AmeriCorps program where I was placed at a local health awareness center in Flint. It was there that I found public health and began to understand what it was. I also learned what health disparities were and how African Americans and other communities of color suffered disproportionately across health indicators whether it was diabetes, stroke, or hypertension. People who looked like me suffered the most. As I began to look at the data it became evident that compared to White Americans, Blacks fared significantly worse across health, education, income, home ownership, etc.

When I took a deeper dive into health disparities and saw that blacks were disproportionately dying, this life changed. I became enraged, infuriated, angry, and focused. Most of these health issues that manifested into disparities were preventable. So, the question for me was, why were we dying at these high rates? Then I was introduced to the social determinants of health and began to understand how housing, transportation, built environment, income, employment, food access, gender culture beliefs, and racism all played a part in the African American experience. Thus, I changed my major and earned a master's and doctorate in public health. I often tell people I did not find public health, public health found me. I believe just as I was called into ministry that I was also called into public health. My calling is a merger of my spiritual lens and my social/cultural lens to meet the needs of the total man (mind, body, and spirit). I endeavor to utilize my public health platform to ensure that people who look like me have equitable access to resources to ensure their overall health and wellness. As stated by the World Health Organization "health is more than the absence of illness and disease." Health for me is multidimensional including physical, mental, environmental, social, cultural, emotional, spiritual, and financial. I often tell others that Jesus, Moses, and Noah were some of the first public health professionals recorded in the Bible.

In 2020, I authored a resolution declaring "Racism a Public Health Crisis" in Genesee County, Michigan. This resolution was passed by the Board of Health and the Board of Commissioners. Declaring racism, a public health crisis suggested the need for a public health response to racism. Racism is a social justice issue that began in the United States in its founding document, the U.S. Constitution. In its original form, it declared slaves and people of African descent as 3/5 of a human being. The founding document that serves as the cornerstone of governance from which our institutions, systems, and governments at all levels operate created this systemic inequity. Later, the constitution was amended regarding African Americans being less than human, that was in "word" only. Yet the institutions, systems, and governmental structures which create systems and policies have not been amended. This is because racism had already been ingrained in the ideologies, belief systems, and mindsets of people, the very people who run our systems, institutions, and governments. This is my public health/social justice issue and I continue to work to dismantle systemic racism and the inequities and disparities it produces.

Beating the Odds: Life Lessons that carried me from Pain to Purpose

Yes, this little boy from Flint, beat the odds. Statistically, being a black boy, with no father, I beat the odds by living past my 18th birthday. I beat the odds by graduating from high school. I beat the odds by not becoming a gang member or drug dealer. I beat the odds by not having an arrest record or seeing a jail or prison. I beat the odds by going to college. I beat the odds by graduating with a bachelor's, master's, and

99

doctorate. I beat the odds by finding my purpose through my pain. How did I do this?

I did this by the grace and strength of God. I learned some tangible lessons along the way that may inspire others.

A.   Your first responsibility in life is to know yourself.

        a.   Embrace those things you consider your strengths, weaknesses, perfections, and imperfections.

        b.   Become comfortable with you are while expecting evolution

        c.   Stand firm in your identity

B.   Your spiritual life is everything.

    a.   Religion is a system, spirituality is a journey

    b.   There is a point in life when you must unlearn what folk have told you about God and you must learn who God is while in relationship

    c.   Embrace activities that feed your spirit and not deplete it

    d.   Know that everything is connected

C.   **Embrace your village** (family, friends, mentors) in all its many forms.

D.   **Be Grateful for your enemies** (they have a role too).

    a.   Some enemies you did not choose or provoke, it's ok. Everyone will not like you.

b.   For the table to be prepared, your enemies must be present. "He will prepare a table before you in the presence of your enemies."

c.   Denial, Betrayal, Lies, and Assassination of Character are all gifts given to us by our enemies, unbeknownst to them.

E.   Never run your race at someone else's pace.

a.   Comparing yourself to others can be deadly: kill your: joy, happiness, drive, desires, and will

F.   Embrace the unknown and align with purpose.

a.   The purpose that was in you before you were born should be the center of all you do, even when it doesn't make sense.

Regina A. Baker, LMSW

Regina has 15 years of experience working in the Social Work field. She also has 10 years of experience working in mental health and substance abuse therapy. Regina earned her Bachelor's Degree at the University of Michigan-Flint and her Master's Degree in Social Work at Michigan State University. Regina is now licensed by the State of Michigan as a Licensed Master Social Worker (LMSW).

Linktree: https://linktr.ee/regina_a_baker_lmsw

A Journey from Anger to Love by
Regina A. Baker, LMSW

Some years ago, my two grandchildren were
put into the foster care system due to abuse and neglect
by their mother, who had a drug abuse problem.
(Their father, my son, was deceased). At one of the
court proceedings, where a decision was being made
about the (care) custody of my grandchildren and with
whom they would reside.

I had a chance to observe conversations and
interactions going on between the social worker,
foster-care worker, CPS worker, and Guardian ad litem
(GAL). Guardian ad litem is a neutral person,
appointed by the court to act in the best interest of the
children. I was struck by how casual the conversations
seemed to be about the children's welfare and I felt
their conversations were void of compassion for the
children's feelings. There was a tug-of-war going on
with the children's mother and the CPS worker. The

mother was defiant towards the CPS worker's requests and began saying, things like "These are my kids and I'll do what I want to with them" The CPS worker was telling the mother that she needed to do as she was asked, and at one point said to the mother "I told you I would get you." At that moment I got angry at all the social workers involved in the case.

I thought to myself, "I can do this job much better and treat these children gentler and show much more compassion for them, also I would let them have a say in their journey." I asked one of the social workers why they didn't ask the children with whom they would like to stay with. The social worker said, "They are not old enough." That is when I learned that there is an age limit of 13 years old before children can have a say in where and with whom they want to live. Now I am angrier. I did get guardianship of my grandchildren. Not once but twice. A couple of years later I was asked again to take custody of them again, for the same reason.

I soon started my social work journey, I was going to be a CPS worker, and I enrolled in Mott Community College, In Flint, Michigan. I worked a full-time job, was a single mother, and went to college part-time it took me about 3 years to finish my associate degree as a Social Work Technician, after graduating from Mott, I enrolled in the University of Michigan-Flint, where I continued to work full time and go to college part-time. I graduated with honors and a bachelor's degree in social work.

I had planned to be done with college after getting my bachelor's degree. Then there was this nagging gut feeling that I should go for my Master's degree because it would make me more marketable in the work field. In 2013, I graduated with honors and my Master's degree, from Michigan State University. That was one of the best decisions I made in my life, with the help of God. "To God be the glory." During my time at the University of Michigan, I changed my mind about becoming a CPS worker. I felt I couldn't stomach taking children from their parents, especially after witnessing that the police must sometimes get involved when there is a threat that violence may occur when the time comes to remove the children from their home. The tears can start flowing from the children's eyes, especially if they're young and don't know why they are being removed from their parents and their home. The children probably wonder what's going on, the garbage bags, (a symbol) where the children's clothes are thrown in hurriedly while removing them from their home.

I volunteered briefly at DHS in Flint where I heard stories of children being removed from their homes and how sometimes it's necessary to have the police involved to prevent any violence. I sat in on some meetings where I learned that one of the main goals of foster care is the reunification of the family if possible. While attending Michigan State University I decided "I am going to be a therapist."

I have a brother named Richard, he was a Vietnam Veteran, who was diagnosed with Schizophrenia shortly after he returned from Vietnam. Richard also played a big role in my decision to become a mental health therapist. I was curious why he acted the way he did sometimes. Richard came to my graduation at Michigan State and told me how proud he was of me.

Thinking back, I recall that at one time, in my life, I was afraid of being around my brother, I didn't understand his mental health or him. Our mother would always take care of Richard, when he'd have a break from reality, usually from not taking his medicine properly. Richard liked to drink alcohol and smoke marijuana and he would end up in a veteran's hospital in whatever city or state he was residing in, such as Atlanta, California, or Florida.

Richard didn't like Michigan because he would say "It's too cold for me" he loved warm weather states. Then in 1988, our mother died. Richard disappeared for a couple of years. I didn't know his whereabouts, then Richard was found one day on the streets of Atlanta Georgia by another veteran, and this gentleman called the Veteran's Administration to have Richard picked up. Richard was hospitalized for months and then one day he called one of our cousins, who then called me to tell me where my brother had been located. I put my social work advocating skills to work for Richard. Richard was flown by the VA back to Flint Michigan, and I took guardianship of him soon after. My brother had to go into an approved locked veteran facility to live, due to his tendency to disappear. My family and I made a promise that he would have the best life possible. Richard loved going to Red Lobster and wearing Jordan tennis shoes and he had both, until he died six years ago.

Presently, I have worked for a non-profit organization for the past 10 years as an LMSW (Licensed Master Social Worker) providing mental health therapy and at times a substance abuse counselor, due to co-occurring diagnoses. Being a Social worker has been the most rewarding and challenging career of my life so far.

Over the past ten years, I've had the pleasure of providing therapy for hundreds of clients, from the age of five and up!

Here are 3 short stories with successful outcomes during my time as a therapist. I remember working with a young lady in her 30s when I first met her. She had a diagnosis of agoraphobia and Generalized Anxiety disorder and lived with her curtains closed all the time. She told me that "I never

open my curtains, and very seldom go outside."
During our therapy time together, I was able to
encourage her to open her curtains and let daylight in.
She eventually went on and enrolled in Mott
Community College, which encouraged me, that I
could make a difference in a person's life. I told her
that I was very proud of her and the courage it took for
her to break the bonds of anxiety. She wrote me a letter
of thanks before she completed outpatient therapy.

Another lady I worked with was very depressed
when I met her, due to the untimely deaths of 2 of her
grandchildren. Since working with her, the depression
she has is now decreasing and she constantly credits me
and God for helping her to look at life differently.

Last is a boy whose mother brought him in at
the age of 13 years old, diagnosed with ADHD,
Autism, and having severe angry outbursts. I just
closed his case in February 2023, he is now 22 years
old, and he said to me one day during therapy "I can

make it on my own now" and asked to be discharged. I felt emotional since we had been together for 9 years. I told him if he ever needed to come back into therapy don't hesitate to come back.

It is great outcomes like these that keep me wanting to do social work. I have so many memorable moments as a social worker. Some memories are sad, tearful, funny, and happy. I've had clients get angry with me, leave my office in a hurry and slam the door.

I am very fortunate to have people respect me enough to put their trust in me to guide their life back on the right track. Now, I have a different outlook about social workers. "I love social workers and have met a lot of great social workers."

I have had the pleasure of supervising two interns and teaching them how to interact when they first encounter a client, how to read body language, and how to turn around a session when it might be going the wrong way. Both young ladies have gone on to become licensed as LMSWs.

One very important thing I do every morning while showering is talk with God about my day. I ask the Lord to guide my day positively and speak through me to any of his children who sit down in front of me if there is anything God wants them to know. Finally, I have opened my own private therapy practice in Flint, Michigan. The name is Cherish Life Therapy and Counseling Services.

Tasha Donald, BS

Tasha Victoria Donald is a longtime resident of Flint, Michigan, with a rich history of over 15 years of serving and empowering individuals and families across Michigan. Her roles have included Adoptions Coordinator, Case Manager, and Youth Mentor. Presently, Tasha serves as a High School At-Risk Coordinator within a local school district. Each day, she works tirelessly alongside various stakeholders, including students, to foster a positive and healthy learning environment.

Beyond her professional roles, Tasha is the CEO and lead facilitator of STYLES: Sophisticated and Tenacious Young Ladies Eager to Succeed. She is a passionate advocate for overall well-being, placing a strong emphasis on mental health, particularly among young ladies and single mothers.

Tasha's dedication extends to her role as a mother to four remarkable young ladies: Jala, Jada, Jordinn, and Journee. Her life's mission is to impart to her daughters the importance of faith and resilience, drawing from her experiences as a young, single mother. Tasha earned her degree from Rochester College in 2007, juggling her studies while raising her twin daughters and a newborn. She teaches her daughters to allow God to be "Big" in their lives and to go through adversity in "Style." Tasha firmly believes that her calling is a divine one, viewing every opportunity as a form of ministry. Whether as a single mother, a survivor of the Flint Water Crisis, a battle with a severe bout of COVID-19, or the daily trials of life, Tasha sees herself as an anointed servant-leader. Her daily mission revolves around impacting as many lives as possible. Even on the most challenging days, when exhaustion sets in and life feels overwhelming,

Tasha remains steadfast in her commitment. She knows she must be the change she wants to see in the world. With determination, she rises each morning, dressed and ready for duty, offering a simple daily request: "Cover Me Lord, I'm Going In."

Tasha is an active member of The Church of God (Kent Street) in Flint, where she serves within the Children and Youth Ministry. She holds a Bachelor of Science degree from Rochester College.

Linktree: https://linktr.ee/tashadonald

A Life of Action by Tasha Donald

As I travel down memory lane, I remember
working with a young, single African-American
mom. She had a beautiful family, but her addiction
and lifestyle brought her under the supervision of the
courts, which led to the removal of her children. I
could not help but consider my own life every time I
touched my case files, but I became extremely sensitive
to this particular case. I, too, was a young mother
trying to find my way, struggling through my
adversities but with no addiction. There was always a
question in the back of my mind concerning this case.
I wondered what led to this mother's addiction and
how I could help pull her out of this dark place. Every
time I interacted with her, I hoped that I could say or
do something that would penetrate her heart and cause
her to rethink her actions. I knew she was hurting, but
her children were suffering too.

Things became clearer after one particular
conversation with this mom. We had just concluded a

supervised visit with her children. I approached her and said, "Mom, I think we need to have a heart to heart. I know you're young and I am too. I know you want to enjoy life, and maybe you weren't ready to give up your freedom to become a mom, but life happened. You have to be willing to stop using drugs and alcohol for your children. Your babies need you! I just know you aren't going to choose habits over your children, are you?" Mom's response was so shocking to me. I'll never forget the words, "I like my drinks and my weed too. You know how it is."

However, I didn't know how it was. It was at this very moment that I believe I was introduced to social work. This mother was plagued with issues far greater than what I realized. Did this mother choose her addiction over her children because something traumatic happened in her past or did she suffer from a mental illness? Could she have been neglected as a child, abused, molested or could she have an undiagnosed or untreated mental health issue? In my opinion, something was preventing her from addressing her addiction issues. She needed support beyond what our agency or I could provide. Meanwhile, her children were placed in separate homes and could only spend time with one another during their once-a-week visitation with their mother. Reality quickly sunk in, as much as I was concerned about this mom, it was the children that I was committed to. I couldn't fail these innocent children. It was my responsibility to ensure they weren't subject to any further negligence. At the time, I was about 25 years old and very new to this life as a Foster Care Worker. Although I lacked experience, I was charged with the unsettling burden to either reunify the children with their parents or to identify a potential adoptive home for them. I soon learned what happy endings were and they could look different depending on the situation. For this particular family, the birth mom's rights were terminated and the siblings were placed in several different adoptive homes, where they would thrive and have permanency.

During my time in child welfare, I was fortunate to finalize over 50 adoptions. I was blessed to play an integral role in children being reunified with their biological families, providing services to prevent the removal of children from their homes, and providing permanency for children. Working in child welfare was the beginning of my journey in the field of social work.

Moving forward a decade, I was blessed to serve at a small non-profit social service agency in Genesee County. The office phones would ring from the time I unlocked the door and disarmed the alarm until the alarm was set at the end of the day. Whether the clients called or came into the office, I never became tired of wearing my big smile and saying, "Good morning/afternoon, how can I help you?" Most of our clients were experiencing some type of personal crisis and it was natural for me to provide exceptional customer service while aiding clients in whatever capacity I could. Our office provided housing financial assistance to those who were facing eviction or those in need of utility assistance. We also offered mailboxes for the homeless and distributed personal hygiene items. It was so rewarding every time I was able to inform clients they qualified for services and to gather the needed documents. I even found pleasure in sorting the mail and coming across the envelopes that our clients were anticipating. I could hardly wait to contact clients and say, "I just sorted the mail, it's here." I think I was as excited as they were. The thought of putting a smile on someone's face and helping others gave me so much fulfillment. It was easy coming to work each day. Deep down inside, I knew that I once walked in my client's shoes, and I knew that I was a paycheck or two away from needing the same services I was providing. Therefore, I was honored to serve.

Shifting from child welfare and social services, I also spent time working in the educational system. I would like to share one of my success stories with one of my students while serving as a behavior specialist. The young man had spent his fair share of time in the Assistant Principal's office and his last referral was the final straw for the Assistant Principal (AP). I remember the AP saying, "Donald, he's going home for the remainder of the school year." I pleaded with him not to suspend the student but to allow me to work with him. I vividly recall the AP looking at me with hesitation, and with my big smile and enormous confidence, I said, "Trust me, I got it."

I connected with that young man for the balance of the school year. Through it all, I mentored, I reminded, and I corrected and not to my surprise, he finished the school year and his behavior significantly improved. On the last day of school, I remember telling the AP, "I told you." It is moments like this that remind me why I show up for duty daily.

I often think, how did I arrive here? While many may have childhood dreams of different careers and others are high school graduates that explore careers and pursue their dreams, I had no clue of what I was destined to do. When I began to pursue my undergraduate degree in Counseling Psychology, I had no idea what I wanted to do or how I would utilize my degree. I had my own young children who were my priority. I wanted to be always readily available to them, but I also knew I had to be a provider. I knew I was passionate about youth, but I had no idea of my career path. Eight months after graduation, I began my work as a child welfare worker serving as a foster care worker, adoption coordinator, and preservation worker. Continuing on my career path, I worked as a family engagement advocate for one of the local Head Start Programs. I soon learned I had an age preference; teens were my niche. The early childhood stages were not my expertise. However, during my employment at Head Start, I was fortunate to participate in Nurturing Parenting Training that would later allow me to facilitate parenting classes for Job Corp participants as well as a cohort of parents at the Cathedral of Faith Head Start Program. This opportunity helped me to realize that I not only was passionate about teens, but I had developed a special love for young mothers. Continuing on my journey, I spent some time working in mental health as a qualified mental health professional in addition to working in the partial hospitalization programs as a group facilitator. I currently serve as an at-risk coordinator, where I can work with a small portion of Genesee County's amazing scholars.

Regardless of the positions I've held, I have been placed in the position to empower, impact, and encourage.

Social work extends across many different sectors, whether in education, social services, mental health, child welfare, or other areas. Social workers directly impact others' quality of life. Social work is more than just a career; It's a lifestyle, and for me it is ministry. Social Work 101 did not teach me to work in this field. This work comes from the innermost part of my heart. It is the love and compassion that God has shown me and has commanded me to have for others. The work that I do may go unseen by others, and I may never become a millionaire by serving and that is okay. My reward is giving others hope and being able to help them during the most challenging times of their lives. Working in this field allows me to get on the battlefield and fight with every individual who's ready to win. I am a frontline warrior! I can serve a diverse population and it is a privilege to do so. I serve because that's what I have been called to do. Rather it's working with a clique of young ladies or a gang of young men standing on the street corner, I want to serve. If I am needed in a severely poverty-stricken community or the beautifully landscaped suburbs, send me, and I will go.

I have received prophecy after prophecy to confirm that I am right where God will have me to be. So, there is nothing more left for me to do, than to "work while it is day, for night cometh and no man can work". God allowed me to survive COVID-19 for a third time, in addition to major health complications, giving me a greater reason to work. "Many is the affliction of the righteous", but I am an example that he will bring you out of them all. God has used my life as an instrument and example of how to turn adversities into triumphs and share my testimonies to help build faith. I rise daily to live out my purpose because I was called to a life of action.

Darcele Marie Cole-Robinson, has been married 31 years to Kenneth Eric Robinson Sr. They have three wonderful children. She has been a long-time native of Genesee County.

Darcele is an educator, entrepreneur, author, publisher, co-author, and anthology author and a co-author of Marriages Ignited Book Anthology and 3 children's books.

She is the founder of the "Donations with Love Foundation" and "Travel with The Robinson. She loves to coordinate events, travel, shop, and do word searches. She also loves to read, watch movies, and plays, and loves spending time with her family.

Linktree: https://linktr.ee/flintrobinson

From Hardship to Victory
By Darcele M. Cole-Robinson, LLMSW

It seemed like it was yesterday, life threw me some mighty tough punches. I lost my sweet mama when I was young, and I had to step up to raise my little sister. It wasn't easy, but I did what I had to do. We built that foundation and made it happen!

I went on to marry my high school sweetheart who is my soulmate, and together, we started a family. But life is not always smooth sailing. I forever lost my in-laws, and I said, "goodbye" to my dear daddy, and my heart broke when we lost one of our own.

Still, I kept my faith strong, trusting in God's love to carry me through. I worked a job for 18 ½ years, loved it, and never missed a day, and one day they were walking all of us out the door. All I ever knew to do was to help people. What was I going to do? At my age, what could I do that I love to do? I decided to go back to school, ASW, BSW, MSW, and now LLMSW. You never know you may call me Dr., I was in a horrific trauma accident when a semi-truck ran into my daughter, and I was rushed to the hospital. I thought I was in a dream and could not wake up!

I felt deep inside that I had to give back to my community and show 'em some love. So, I started "Donations with Love," a nonprofit where I could lend a hand to individuals who needed it the most. I believed that love and support could change lives for the better. Our motto: When we refresh others through giving, we refresh ourselves.

I found strength in my faith and my Baptist roots. I believed God had a plan for me, and my calling was clear as day. I wanted to make a difference, to lend a hand to those in need, just like He did for me.

But life has not always been a bed of roses and sunshine. A fire came crashing down, and I almost lost it all. I was ready to throw in the towel, but a miracle came when they saved my hard drive. It was like God was saying, "Girl get up!" "Keep going, child. I have you."

I refused to let that fire beat me down. I saw it as a chance to find my calling again. My husband and I worked together to make it through this process. I knew deep down that I had a purpose to fulfill.

With my man right by my side, we continued our journey together "Traveling with the Robinsons," spreading joy and making memories with everyone. We love to see smiling faces.

But the fire inside me wasn't still burning. I knew I could do more. I wanted to support my community and be there for those who needed it most. So, I became a social worker, determined not to make a real impact. I have written children's books, and devotional anthologies and worked to help eliminate stigma, poverty, and illiteracy.

As a Family Coach, help those families recover and heal through their process knowing all the trauma their loved ones have struggled with some type of substance. It's all about LOVE!

Through all the hardships, I found my way to victory. My family, my love for God, and my community kept me going. I showed the world that no matter what life throws at you, you can rise above it. "I RISE". Seeing your setback as a setup for your COMEBACK!

In coming out of your setbacks, your "could've, should've, or would've," should only be seen as a grieving part of your setback and not the end of your dreams, hopes, and goals.

Nevertheless, to find out why it's so important to come out of your setback into your comeback, you must become willing to allow God to rearrange your surroundings, your circle of friends, and or the way you do some things.

My journey from struggle to success inspires others to believe in themselves and in the power of lending a helping hand. I found my purpose, and now

I'm spreading love and compassion wherever I go. And that, my friends, is what love is all about. When you like Joseph, you find yourself in a pit but know God's got you in his plans.

Marcus Batson

M. D. Batson has served youth and families affected by abuse and trauma for over a decade. Additionally, he has worked as an advocate for youth and transition-aged young adults, including former foster youth, to help improve their outcomes for successful living. M.D. Batson is also an experienced workshop presenter, public speaker, and ordained minister.

Informed by Experience

By Marcus Batson

Working with young people has been an unequivocal joy in my life. They possess a unique, almost blissful, sense of unawareness, often filled with boundless dreams and aspirations. Their hopes console me, and their dreams invigorate my passion. Over the course of my career, I've, like many other well-meaning adults, asked the children of our future, "What do you want to be when you grow up?" As the number of youths, I've engaged with has increased, certain aspirations have emerged as typical responses: professional athletes, business leaders or entrepreneurs, teachers, doctors, lawyers, accountants, skilled tradespeople, and even police officers. Yet, some simply shrug and say, "I don't know." I've heard a myriad of responses, but there's one answer that has remained conspicuously absent: "I want to be a social worker when I grow up."

My professional journey in social work spans almost a dozen years, but in reality, I've been engaged with the social work target population for much longer. Like the young people I've tirelessly queried about their future endeavors, the idea of social work was never part of my initial life plan. Instead, I had envisioned myself as a teacher, a guiding light for students who, like me, grew up in challenging circumstances. I pictured a slender, smooth-faced figure, sporting a mid-flat top haircut, clad in a green button-up shirt with a tie – a philosophical teacher navigating the complexities of life in the hood, not unlike Furious Styles from the film "Boyz n the Hood." It was this vision that accompanied my daydreams about the future.

Perhaps my formative years, marked by attendance at eighteen different schools, including an astonishing three different schools each year from first through fifth grade, played a substantial role in shaping my imagination. But life had other plans for me. High school assessments pointed me toward a future in courier work, and upon entering college, I boldly declared a business major. However, a humbling experience in a Business Calculus course, which the university claimed I was qualified for, quickly altered my course. In a move I still don't fully comprehend to this day, I switched my undergraduate focus to social work.

My story, as I perceive it, transcends the realm of employment. Oddly enough, I'd prefer to spend my days delivering packages, working in solitude while listening to the soothing tunes of gospel or jazz. It's the experiences, etched deeply into the tapestry of my life, that have convinced me that social work is my true calling. In many ways, it feels as if I've been ordained to serve families, harbor unwavering compassion for young people, and stand with individuals during some of the most arduous times in their lives. Over the years, as I've helped others navigate the labyrinth of their experiences, elements from my own past have coalesced in a manner that has solidified my belief that this work is my true vocation for this specific era of my life.

No one could have foreseen that I would have to grapple to remain on this path. In hindsight, the social work environment surrounded me throughout my upbringing. As a former foster youth, I encountered the instability of moving from one home to another, yearning for a sense of stability and belonging. I spent the first week of my tenth birthday in an adolescent psychiatric hospital, an experience that no child should ever endure. Later, I discovered that some of my high school friends' parents were social workers, individuals undoubtedly privy to the challenges I was navigating.

A pivotal moment occurred when a friend I interviewed for a social work project unveiled their innermost motivation for delivering exceptional service on the job: "Our families deserve to be serviced by a professional." This seemingly simple yet profoundly powerful sentiment became a lodestar for my career. It dawned on me that providing excellent service was not merely a personal ambition; it was a moral obligation. This lesson has remained the cornerstone of my journey, compelling me to be the consummate professional that our families rightfully deserve. Nearly two decades later, I still vividly recall that statement.

My undergraduate experience in social work was marked by exceptional challenges. A maelstrom of inexperience, an imbalance between work, school, and life, and other personal issues led to a disheartening outcome. I failed nearly every class during my first senior year, and I believe I may have passed only one semester of my fieldwork class. I was on the brink of giving up and dropping out of school, despite being the recipient of an academic scholarship. I had grown disillusioned with the conventional classroom setting, and I had no desire to implore the social work department to allow me to remain in the program, retaking all of those classes as a probationary student.

Fortunately, circumstances took an unexpected turn. The people who had supported me thus far reminded me that I owed it to others, if not to myself, to finish what I had started. Despite feeling like a beggar at the time, I officially requested a meeting with the department heads, imploring them to permit me to continue in the program. I willingly accepted their terms of probation, even taking out student loans to cover the costs of classes I had previously taken. This phase of my life taught me the enduring value of perseverance, the profound importance of seeing commitments through, and the transformative role of unwavering support from loved ones.

I eventually graduated and embarked on my professional journey. The details of my odyssey could fill an entire book. To say that I encountered difficult decisions and learned hard lessons early on, all for the privilege of facing secondary trauma daily through my work, gives me reason to pause. I've come to understand that the work drawn to me operates in cycles; just when you feel you've made a difference in someone's life, two more individuals with similar needs and challenges step into your world.

Working in a field as emotionally demanding as social work has reinforced the significance of self-care and coping mechanisms. Over time, I've developed an arsenal of strategies to safeguard my mental and emotional well-being. These include taking breaks to recharge, seeking solace and guidance from colleagues, and discovering solace in the soothing rhythms of music. These practices have proven indispensable in preserving my equilibrium in a field that frequently exposes me to the secondary trauma experienced by those I endeavor to assist.

In essence, my journey as a social worker transcends the sphere of employment. It's a testament to the lives I've touched, the adversities I've faced, and the invaluable lessons I've internalized. It's a narrative of unwavering resilience, boundless compassion, and an enduring commitment to serving those in need.

Through the labyrinthine trials and tribulations, I've discovered my true purpose, understanding that the work continually drawn to me unfolds in cycles, a perpetual journey of extending a helping hand, empowering others, and etching an enduring impact on the lives of those I encounter.

Ayana Marie Fordham, MA, LCSW

Who is Ayana Marie Fordham?

I'm a mother, a spiritually grounded Licensed Clinical Social Worker (LCSW) with experience transforming trials into testimonies. I'm a native of Flint, MI currently living in Tokyo, Japan. I've learned to "Live Life on Purpose with Purpose." I would concede that I embrace my truths most days, accepting my strengths as well as my weaknesses. I'm an active member of The Everlasting Baptist Church, the National Association of Social Workers (NASW), National Association for the Advancement of Colored

People (NAACP), Zeta Phi Beta Sorority, Incorporated, Omega Theta Zeta Chapter, and The Order of the Eastern Star, Electa Chapter No.25 Okinawa, Japan.

As a champion, a survivor of both childhood and adult life adverse experiences I'm resilient embracing opportunities to share my story in hopes of encouraging others. I'm evidence that resiliency is formed through adversity. I possess a Master of Social Worker degree from Michigan State University, as well as a Master of Arts degree in Organizational Management from Spring Arbor University. I have 20+ years of combined human service & social work experience; servicing adults, children, families, and communities in medical, military, educational, substance-abuse, & community-based settings. I hold high esteem for the populations I serve and my colleagues. Many of my successes in life came with the support of the people I was working with at the time. I'm dedicated to providing quality service with integrity. My personal and professional experiences have proven that respect is a key element of healthy relationships, but more important how I treat myself is how others learn how to treat me. This is probably why I am my biggest critic and fan all at the same time.

As a clinical social worker, I promote mental wellness through advocacy, psychoeducation, and psychotherapy. I enjoy helping others transform their life challenges into healthy lifestyle changes.

In March 2021 I was featured in Courageous Women Magazine a U.S.-based magazine and was a participant on the magazine's Podcast on Club House in late April 2021. I was a special guest on the Tynee Talks Podcast, in Dallas, Texas in early May 2021, and I've written articles for AmaGra Magazine in Bradenton, FL.

Seeking opportunities to promote effective change and mental wellness to individuals through direct care services, speaking engagements, and literary work is who I am. I believe that change takes time but is possible. My company, KlockWise, Inc. is based on the fundamental principles of its acronym K.L.O.C.K. W.I.S.E., Knowledge, Loyalty, Opportunity, Courage, Kindness, Wisdom, Integrity, Support, & Empowerment. God's Word and Promises assure me that I'm extended Grace daily which allows me to acknowledge my past, be active in my present, and make preparation for my future. It's my prayer that I'm making a positive difference and extending Grace to others. My personal and professional experiences have proven that "Resiliency is Powerful, how we overcome in our lives and what we do to help others overcome in their lives matters."

Linktree: https://linktr.ee/fordhamayana

Say G.R.A.C.E.

By Ayana M Fordham, MA, LCSW

For many of us as a child, Grace went a little something like this, "God is good, God is great, let us thank Him for our food Amen!" We were taught to give thanks to God for our meals. As a social worker, a licensed clinician, and an adult woman saying Grace is my way of thanking God for everything. To "Say Grace" is my way of resetting myself when life seems difficult. As a social worker, "Say Grace" is my restoration, my healing, my reminder, my way of returning to a state of service and gratitude.

Often people ask what is Grace? Well, when people say, "Thank God, I don't look like what I've been through;" that's GRACE. That unmerited favor we receive in our lives every day. Personally, I'm not sure where I would be today, had it not been for Grace. My life has been inundated with adverse experiences, both as a child and an adult. I'm no stranger to trauma. Many have tried to diminish my value and question my abilities. When I was twelve years old, an adult told me "I would never amount to anything." They were wrong. Grace has taught me that I am somebody and I am valued. Grace has shown me the importance of being silent and not reacting or responding to the nay-sayers. I've learned to confuse them with silence and "Enlighten" them with my actions. I was inspired as a child by my maternal grandmother who was also a social worker. She taught me that our actions & words matter. What we do and say during times of tribulation is impactful. She taught me prayer is unconditional and necessary. She taught me about Grace and showed me the joy of being a social worker.

Being a Licensed Clinical Social Worker is a continuous journey. It's a journey filled with transforming pain into purpose. I find that it's all worth it because of Grace.

If I'm honest, many of my personal and professional successes and failures have been influenced by Grace extended to me by others. On Dec. 6, 2012, my life took a major shift when my mother passed away. There I was entering the final semester of my Master of Social Work program at Michigan State University consumed by grief. Unsure how to move forward. Some people thought I was "okay" because I had worked in the social work field for years, I was in graduate school, and I had always been there for everyone around me. I guess that meant I was supposed to be exempt from grieving. It was the opposite, I wasn't okay, I was giving up and I dropped out of school. Thankful to my daughter, family, friends, a few classmates, and my instructors who supported me, I graduated with honors. Now, fast forward to Sunday, Oct 27, 2013, the day life threw me another curve ball. That was the day I drove myself to the emergency room only to learn I was having a stroke, and I was ultimately diagnosed with Multiple Sclerosis at the same time. I thought to myself "Lord are You serious right now!" I didn't know what to do, but once again the Lord together with my village of family, friends, and colleagues extended me Grace. These life-changing events made me question my purpose, yet they resurrected my faith, my belief in prayer, and my appreciation for the people in my life. There it was GRACE, teaching me that I was resilient, and I wasn't alone. It was GRACE teaching me that there was praise in the acceptance of my past, purpose in my present, and how to be intentional with my future. Grace reassured me that our perspectives matter.

You see, to "Say Grace" for me is to be thankful for all I've overcome, to reset and restore who I am as a clinician, a person, and a Believer. It's my self-care, my motivation, my WHY. To "Say Grace" is to acknowledge my resiliency & live in my truths. Psalm 51:12 says, "Restore to me the joy of your salvation, and uphold me with a willing spirit." We know that God extends Grace to us daily.

However, we often neglect to extend GRACE to ourselves and others. Grace is an essential part of life; it brings stability to our mental wellbeing. It's healing, it's hope, its forgiveness, it's Favor. Through my work as a Social Worker, I strive to incorporate GRACE in the services I provide. I can only hope that I am empowering others to find GRACE within themselves.

GRACE is "Gratitude, Resiliency, Acceptance, & Empowerment." There is gratitude in our service, purpose in our actions, power in accepting our truths, and resiliency through empowerment. Remember there is power in the tongue, when you feel discouraged & life is "lifing," move in silence and just,

"Say Grace!"

Dedicated to my grandmother Mattie L.
Fordham, BSW

Made in the USA
Coppell, TX
06 January 2024

27298065R10085